Days Out Around Cocoa Beach

Gillian Birch

Cover Photo: Courtesy RWB

ISBN-10: 1514148072

ISBN-13: 978-1514148075

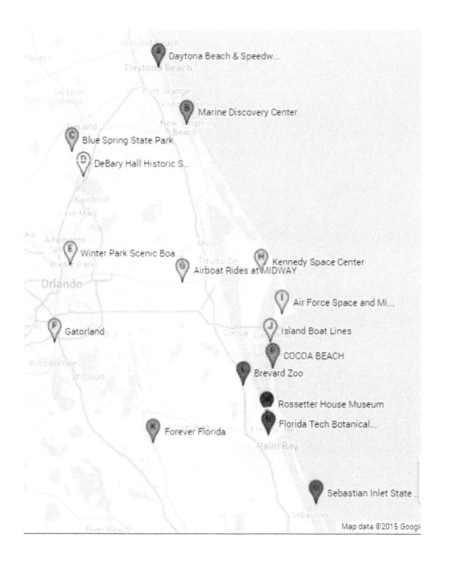

Key

- Daytona Beach & Speedway
- Marine Discovery Center
- Blue Spring State Park
- DeBary Hall
- Winter Park Scenic Boat Tour
- Gatorland
- Airboat Rides at Midway
- Kennedy Space Center
- Air Force Space and Missile ...
- Island Boat Lines
- Forever Florida
- Brevard Zoo
- Rossetter House Museum
- FloridaTech Botanical Gardens
- Sebastian Inlet State Park
- COCOA BEACH

CONTENTS

An Introduction to Cocoa Beach

Beautiful Cocoa Beach is a coastal city of around 11,000 residents in Brevard County. Frequently referred to as "Orlando's local beach", it is just 60 miles east of the international tourist mecca. This makes Cocoa Beach a popular destination for enjoying a relaxing beach and watersports vacation within easy reach of Orlando's theme parks and shopping malls.

Cocoa Beach is a pleasant community boasting six miles of beautiful sandy beaches, a fishing pier, 27-hole public golf course, three oceanfront parks and a host of dining establishments and attractions including Ron Jon's, the largest surf shop in the world.

From NASA to NASCAR

Located on Florida's Space Coast, the area has some unique attractions such as the Kennedy Space Center, the Astronaut Hall of Fame and the historic Air Force Space and Missile Museum. This is the only place in the world where you can tour the facilities of past, present and future space travel. You may even be lucky enough to get a grandstand view of a satellite or rocket launch during your stay!

If you're into speed, you can enjoy a behind-the-scenes tour at the Daytona International Speedway, which is within easy reach of Cocoa Beach. The firm sands of Daytona Beach, where NASCAR racing first began, now provide opportunities for surfing, walking, sunbathing, swimming and fishing.

Water and Wildlife

The lagoons and Intracoastal Waterway provide a fun way to see Florida's unique wildlife and birds on scenic boat tours and exhilarating airboat rides. Explore the lakes and canals around Winter Park or cruise gently down the Banana River exploring the Thousand Islands Conservation Area on a leisurely eco tour with a local naturalist.

The warm waters at Blue Spring State Park provide refuge for many endangered manatees, while Gatorland hosts excellent animal shows with some of Florida's more prolific wildlife. However, the best way to see native flora and fauna in a natural setting is on a relaxing horseback safari through the 4,700-acre conservancy at Forever Florida's Crescent J Ranch.

You can get up-close to more exotic animals with a day at the Brevard Zoo, or visit the Marine Discovery Center at New Smyrna Beach and take a thrilling dolphin tour. Join a guided kayaking eco safari, take a boat tour with a marine scientist in the Indian River Lagoon or observe hermit crabs, seahorses, starfish and anemones in the aquariums and touch tanks at this excellent free attraction.

Museums and Historic Homes
Those who enjoy history will not want to miss the Rossetter House Museum, which offers guided tours of two of the oldest historic homes in the Eau Gallie area of Melbourne.

More history can be found at the lavishly furnished DeBary Hall, a former plantation on the banks of the St Johns River. Tales of riverboats, hunting parties and Victorian life on an orange grove come vividly to life at this estate home, which is now listed on the National Register of Historic Places.

Just south of Cocoa Beach, the McLarty Treasure Museum tells the story of shipwreck and lost treasure. This fascinating museum is on the site of a Survivors Camp after a fleet of Spanish galleons sank just offshore in a hurricane in 1715. Along with the Sebastian Fishing Museum, it is part of the Sebastian Inlet State Park, another fantastic amenity for visitors and residents of Cocoa Beach to enjoy.

Insider Info on Cocoa Beach

These diverse attractions and fun things to do around Cocoa Beach are just a taste of what this book has in store. Written by a Florida local, this informative guide book offers readers the chance to discover more off-the-beaten path attractions. It includes detailed descriptions, photographs, and tips for free tours and ideas for family days out that won't break the budget. What's more, all the suggested trips are less than 85 miles from Cocoa Beach, and many are right on your doorstep.

Packed with information on where to eat and what to do, this book is a must for anyone visiting Cocoa Beach. Each chapter is a descriptive reference source that makes easy armchair reading for anyone planning to visit Central Florida. It's like visiting Cocoa Beach hand-in-hand with your own local guide, enriching your vacation experience, and saving you time and money.

Happy trails!

What's What

Introduction: Each destination begins with a short description of the attraction and what it offers, to help you choose a day out that will best suit your needs.

Location: Full address, contact details and location make getting to each attraction very easy.

Directions: Distances are all calculated from the A1A/Minutemen Causeway. Most destinations are less than an hour's drive from Cocoa Beach.

What to Expect: This section gives a full and detailed description of what the attraction has to offer, including guided tours, personal tips, best times to visit and other pertinent information for you to get the most from your visit.

Where to Eat: These are all family-friendly places that I have personally experienced and would happily go back to. The businesses did not know I was gathering information for a book; I was simply there as an ordinary paying customer.

Cost: Admission prices and cost of boat trips, guided tours etc. are all correct at time of going to press in early 2015. They are intended as a guideline only and may be subject to change in the future.

Opening Times: I have supplied general information, telephone numbers and website links. It is advisable to call and confirm details before setting off, to avoid disappointment.

Nearby Attractions: Once you have enjoyed visiting your chosen destination, other nearby attractions are suggested to extend your day out or include as a detour on your journey home.

Sebastian Inlet State Park and Museums

Sebastian Inlet State Park is Mother Nature's theme park with a host of things to see and do for all ages. Chill out on the 3-mile beach or go shelling, surfing and fishing. The park caters admirably for energetic youngsters, divers, cyclists, anglers, birdwatchers, hikers, boaters, kayakers, geocachers, picnickers and families, providing excellent amenities.

This historic site on Florida's Treasure Coast is home to two museums. Learn about the history of three early settler families who ran a fishing industry in Sebastian Inlet. See the replica fish house and dock along with a collection of exhibits about local history.

The neighboring McLarty Treasure Museum is on the site of the survivors' camp from the Spanish fleet that was shipwrecked there in 1715. An exciting movie tells the story of the stricken vessels, and how archaeologists and salvagers continue to unearth the fleet's treasures.

A little history, a tale of lost treasure, miles of scenic trails and a gorgeous beach – what more can you wish for from this excellent state park attraction near Cocoa Beach.

Location
Located 51 miles south of Cocoa Beach on the A1A

Sebastian Inlet State Park
9700 South Highway A1A
Melbourne Beach
FL 32951
Tel: (321) 724-5424

www.floridastateparks.org/park/Sebastian-Inlet

What to Expect on a Visit to Sebastian Inlet State Park
Sebastian Inlet State Park is easy to reach on a scenic drive down the A1A. The two-lane highway runs down the chain of barrier islands separating the Atlantic Ocean beaches from the calm Indian River waterway.

Sebastian Inlet State Park is a manmade cut between the barrier islands, connecting the ocean with the unspoiled Indian River Lagoon.

The park covers over 1,000 acres with an outstanding range of recreational opportunities on the beautiful sandy beach, intracoastal shoreline and inland hammock where birds, fish and wildlife abound.

Activities and amenities on offer at Sebastian Inlet State Park include:

- Three miles of golden sandy beach
- Walks along the mile-long Hammock Trail enjoying birds, squirrels, lizards and small mammals that live in the subtropical palm-oak hammock
- 10-mile Volksport Hiking Trail starting at the Inlet concession
- Swimming (no lifeguards on duty but red flags indicate dangerous currents and undertow). The Cove provides shallow safe water for children to splash and swim
- Excellent surfing along the Atlantic coastline. Surf breaks can be found near the North Jetty and at Monster Hole
- Bicycling on three paved and off-road trails for mountain bikes totaling 40 miles. All trails start and end at the marina
- Fishing from the catwalk and jetties
- Snorkeling and scuba diving, exploring miles of rocky reefs just offshore
- Birdwatching on part of the Great Florida Birding and Wildlife Trail within the park. Bird Checklists are available from Park Rangers
- Wildlife Viewing – look out for dolphins, nesting sea turtles, manatees and other marine life in the area
- Boating, kayaking and canoeing through the mangroves from the Inlet Marina boat ramps. Rentals are available

- Geocaching – download the official tracking sheet clues from geocaching.com and start hunting for your own "treasure"
- Children's playground with swings, slides and a big green dinosaur!
- Interpretive exhibits about turtles and other local information
- Overnight camping and restroom facilities
- Restaurant, gift shop and bait shop open daily
- Ranger-led tours by prior arrangement

As if all this is not enough, the historic site of a shell midden and a shipwreck survivors' camp provide plenty of exciting local history in the two museums onsite.

McLarty Treasure Museum

Housed in a building donated by Mr. Robert McLarty, this fascinating museum occupies the former site of the Survivors and Salvagers' Camp 1715 Fleet.

Now a National Historical Landmark, this museum is manned by volunteers. It tells the story of 11 treasure galleons of the Spanish Fleet attempting to return to Spain laden with treasure from Mexico when they sank just offshore in a hurricane.

The exhibits include weapons, a helmet and breastplate worn by Spanish soldiers and replicas of treasure recovered from shipwrecks in the area. Cannonballs, tools, pistols, bottles, pottery, coins, a ship's bell and precious metal ingots make up the well-laid out displays.

It's well worth escaping the heat for a time and watching the movie *The Queen's Jewels and the 1715 Fleet* which is played continuously in the museum. It tells the tale of how 1500 survivors from the fleet struggled ashore to await rescue in improvised shelters, but many died of exhaustion and exposure.

Help eventually arrived from the Spanish settlement in St Augustine, quickly followed by salvagers, pirates, divers and looters looking to find themselves some bounty from the seabed.

The shipwreck was rediscovered in 1928. Spanish artifacts marking the site of the survivors' camp were discovered in the early 1940s and more treasures were recovered through the 1960s. Further archaeological research suggests that the middens and shell mounds found on the site were probably from the sizeable 16th century Ais Indian settlement.

Sebastian Fishing Museum

This is an informative museum dedicated to the history and culture of Sebastian's fishing industry. History is told through the lives of three local families: the Semblers, Smiths and Judahs.

See a hand-built fishing boat, a replica fishhouse, nets, fishing gear and old photographs.

State Park Admission

$8 per vehicle with up to 8 occupants
$4 Single occupant vehicle
$2 Pedestrians and cyclists

McLarty Treasure Museum Admission
Adults and children over the age of 6 $2

Sebastian Fishing Museum Admission
Included in park entry fees

Opening Times
Sebastian Inlet State Park is open 24 hours a day, 365 days a year.

Both museums are open daily from 10 a.m. to 4 p.m. excluding major holidays.

Where to Eat at Sebastian Inlet State Park
The park has a number of picnic tables and pavilions for picnics.

The Inlet Grill is a modern two-story snack shack serving hot breakfast platters, hot dogs, Mahi sandwiches, basket meals, seafood, tacos and ice cream at reasonable prices throughout the day. The second floor balcony has great views of the park and there is air-conditioned seating available inside.

Other nearby restaurants outside the state park include Mo-Bay Grill on Indian River Drive and The Italian Cousin just south of Sebastian Inlet State Park on US-1.

Nearby Attractions
- Brevard Zoo
- Rossetter House Museum
- Florida Tech Botanical Gardens

Botanical Garden at Florida Institute of Technology

Nicknamed "The Jungle" by students of Florida Tech, this is one of the most unique botanical gardens in Florida. Free to visit, this tropical hammock has over 200 palm species, ferns, bamboos and native flowers. It covers 15 acres beside the Indian River and includes the historic Little Red Schoolhouse. The gardens are a haven for wildlife such as frogs, turtles, butterflies, birds and raccoons.

More a palm forest than a botanical garden, these well-maintained public gardens are a delightful place to visit. Allow about an hour and enjoy a shady walk through the tropical greenery beside the trickling waters of Crane Creek. Benches, pergolas and shady gazebos are scattered throughout the gardens providing tranquil places to relax and enjoy the natural serenity.

If you are interested in identifying the many different established palms, you can download a self-guided walking tour from the Florida Institute of Technology website below.

Location

Located 22 miles south of Cocoa Beach in the campus of Florida Institute of Technology (FIT) in Melbourne.

Botanical Garden
Florida Institute of Technology
150 West University Blvd
Melbourne
FL32901
Tel: (386) 668-3840

http://garden.fit.edu/

What to Expect on a Visit to the Botanical Garden at FIT

Start your visit by entering the campus gardens on the south side from South Babcock Street, opposite the Evans Library. The path leads around to the small red hut which was Melbourne's first schoolhouse.

Erected in 1883 by settler John Goode, black and white students were taught in this historic building by Maude Goode and May Valentine. There was no space for desks in the 9 by 12 foot building, so students sat on long benches and wrote on slates.

The school only operated in the summer and apparently a hand pump stood outside the door providing drinking water to the students. The Little Red Schoolhouse was relocated to the gardens in 1971 from its original site on Fountain Heights (South Riverview Drive) on the Indian River.

Continue along the main Dent Smith Trail, which was named after the Palm Specialist who founded the Palm Society and grew many species at his home in Daytona Beach. His expert knowledge, generosity and inspiration helped make the gardens possible.

Originally, around 400 species of palms found their way into this Botanical Garden, but severe winter freezes killed off the less hardy species, leaving the substantial collection of mature trees and exotic plants that survives today. Many of the original trees are still marked with their silver identification tags.

Exploring this delightful dense native hardwood hammock, you will pass the Heart of Palm Garden on your left. Where the trail divides, you will see a rare Choco Palm (Mexico) surrounded by showy canna lilies. The main trail continues around to the left, crossing the creek several times over pretty bridges to reach the Turtle Pond and connect with the Bamboo Trail near Grissom Hall.

Return to the trail junction and explore the Creek Branch Loop, a circular route with a detour off around the Teardrop Garden of specimen trees. Look out for the Spiny Liculala Palms (Indonesia) with their segmented circular leaves on the loop. At the far end of the garden is a delightful Butterfly Garden.

Main highlights of the gardens include the trio of Gingerbread Palms (Africa) with oval fruits which have a distinctive ginger flavor. Around the Dent Smith Trail Stone Marker are several Bottle Palms (Mascarene Islands), a magnificent Staghorn Fern in a hanging planter and a tall Royal Palm which loves the swampy area near the creek's floodplain.

The gardens have several Sabal Palms (Cabbage Palms) which are the Florida state tree and Florida's only native palm tree. The tender center provides the "heart of palm" used in salads, but harvesting this delicacy kills the tree.

The Fishtail Palms (SE Asia) are easily identified by their spreading fishtail leaves and the climbing giant Philodendron (Swiss Cheese Plant) from Brazil also has easily identified split leaves. A variety of striking bamboos and a Traveler's Palm (Madagascar) complete the Upper Walk.

Additional Information

To preserve the gardens, dogs, bicycles and skateboards are not allowed. For safety reasons, children should be supervised.

Admission

Free

Opening Times

Open daily sunrise to sunset.

Where to Eat near the Botanical Garden at FIT

Meg O'Malley's is a popular bar and Irish pub on East New Haven Ave less than two miles from FIT. It serves excellent food, classic Irish favorites and specialty ice creams for dessert along with draft beers, Guinness and ciders. You may want to linger and enjoy the live evening entertainment at this popular downtown restaurant.

Nearby, The Mansion is a restaurant deli and bakery with wonderful river views from the Upper Terrace. It's a good choice for a special meal or romantic dinner, with high quality food and flavorsome dishes.

Nearby Attractions

- Brevard Zoo
- Sebastian Inlet State Park
- Rossetter House Museum and Gardens

Rossetter House Museum and Gardens

Listed on the Register of Historic Places, the charming Rossetter House Museum and Gardens provides an entertaining way to spend time learning about local settler history. You can walk around the gardens and admire the exterior of the house without charge, but to get the most from your visit, you need to book a place on the fascinating guided tour.

Rossetter House courtesy TropicArt

The family history is intrinsically linked to the neighboring Houston Family Cemetery and the Roesch House opposite, now used as the Museum Offices and Gift Shop.

Discover more about the joys and sorrows of the Houston/Rossetter family as you step back in time in this beautifully furnished period home.

Location
Located 15 miles south of Cocoa Beach in the Eau Gallie Arts District of Melbourne.

Rossetter House Museum
1320 Highland Avenue
Melbourne
FL32935
Tel: (321) 254-9855

www.rossetterhousemuseum.org

What to Expect on a Visit to Rossetter House Museum
Parking for visitors to the Rossetter House Museum is on the north side of the gardens, on Hector Street. Tours begin at the two-story Roesch House on Highland Ave, opposite the gracious Rossetter Mansion.

These historic local properties are managed by the Florida Historical Society in conjunction with the Rossetter House Foundation. They include the 1908 James Wadsworth Rossetter House and Gardens, the 1901 Roesch House and the earlier 1865 Houston Family Memorial Cemetery.

Roesch House now serves as the Museum HQ and includes the charming Ella's Closet Gift Shop. Guided tours begin in the parlor with a short introduction to the family and more general pioneer history of the area.

The tour moves on to the Houston Family Cemetery nearby with just 12 graves marked by unusual head and footstones.

The highlight of the docent-led tour is visiting the beautifully restored Rossetter House Mansion and learning about the Rossetter family, who arrived in Melbourne in 1902. All the furnishings are original family pieces, from the chamber pot beneath the bed to the Victorian brass birdcage complete with tweeting bird!

Originally this area, known as Eau Gallie, was covered in sugar cane, rice and citrus groves. It later became the southern point of Flagler's East Coast Railroad. The Houston Family were the first settlers in the area in 1859 and had the first home on the site where the Rossetter House now stands. John Carroll Houston operated a staging post on the river during the Civil War and later served as a Brevard Commissioner. His daughter Ada Louise Houston married William Roesch in 1885, hence the family connection between the two historic homes and the cemetery.

William Roesch was an early land developer, the local mayor, postmaster and founder of the local newspaper, *The Eau Gallie Record*. Sadly, five of their six children died between 1887 and 1895 and are buried in the family cemetery.

When James Rossetter developed the gracious family mansion on Highland Ave in 1908, the area already had a hotel and bustling commercial district on the banks of the Indian River. Rossetter worked as a merchant in the fishing industry and established himself as an agent for Rockefeller's Standard Oil Company.

The original home was expanded when Rossetter purchased the former winter home of John Aspinwall. He moved it to its current site to create the west wing of Rossetter House.

In 1921, James Rossetter died, leaving his eldest daughter Caroline (Carrie) in charge of the business at the age of 23. Carrie and her sister Ella lived in the house all their lives. The sisters eventually bequeathed the property, furnishings and treasured contents to the Rossetter House Foundation to be preserved as a historic legacy of life in early Eau Gallie.

The tour ends in the gardens with the chance to admire the vintage Ford Model A automobile that once belonged to Ella Rossetter. The extensive lawned gardens are edged with palms, live oaks and staghorn ferns. Shady patios and attractive water features make this a popular venue for weddings and private events.

Additional Information
Docent-led tours start on the hour and last for 45-60 minutes. Reservations are not usually necessary.

Special events at the historic home museum include an Easter Egg Hunt, Ghost Tours and a popular Murder Mystery Tour which takes place three times a year.

Admission and Tour
Guided tours are $8 per person.

Opening Times
Open Wednesday through Saturday 11a.m. to 4 p.m.

Where to Eat near Rossetter House Museum

There are several places to dine in the historic Eau Gallie Arts District of downtown Melbourne.

Chef Mario's Italian Café Restaurant offers casual gourmet dining with a tempting menu ranging from stone oven-baked pizzas to delicious fresh mussels.

Concepts on Highland has a good choice of salads, steaks and seafood in the historic atmosphere of the Old Bank building of Eau Gallie.

Nearby Attractions

- Botanical Gardens at FIT
- Brevard Zoo
- Sebastian Inlet State Park

Brevard Zoo and Treetop Trek

Brevard Zoo advertises itself as a little zoo that does big things, and it's true. The emphasis at the zoo is on experiencing a variety of wildlife and having some unique adventures, all reinforcing a message of Conservation through Education and Participation.

As well as a range of interactive wildlife experiences and adventures, the zoo offers a self-guided aerial obstacle course with zip lines as part as part of the separate Treetop Trek.

Location
Located in north Melbourne across the Pineda Causeway (Hwy 404) from Cocoa Beach

Brevard Zoo and Treetop Trek
8225 North Wickham Road
Melbourne
FL32940
Tel: (321) 254-9453

https://brevardzoo.org

www.treetoptrek.com

What to Expect on a Visit to Brevard Zoo
This modern well-planned zoo is set on 50 acres and has over 500 animals with 130+ different species. The animals are divided into various "lands" such as Expedition Africa, Australia and Asia, Wild Florida, La Selva Rainforest and Paws On.

Feeding the giraffes is one of the highlights in Expedition Africa as they approach and extend their long necks to take the offered leaf, displaying their long black tongue. Rhinos, antelopes, camels, impalas, cute lemurs, exotic birds and gangly ostriches can all be seen in this exciting area.

You will find some of the world's most unusual animals in the Australia Asia land where kangaroos and wallabies bound around. Colorful cassowaries, plump kookaburras and squawking parrots make a lively display and there's also the chance to hand feed the brightly colored rainbow lorikeets. Gibbons from Asia can also be seen swinging from trees and generally showing off to visitors.

Wild Florida is a home-from-home for the alligators, crocodiles, flamingoes, otters, wolves, turtles, Sandhill cranes and birds of prey that make this zone their home. The best way to discover them in their natural environment is by kayaking across the wetland area.

Monkeys, vultures, beautifully coated jaguars, scaly anteaters, sloths, tapirs, tamarinds, tortoises and toucans abound in the South American La Selva zone.

Paws On provides more interactive animal experiences with a Lagoon Aquarium, Turtle Beach and Upland Area where gopher tortoises hang out. Pet some of the animals, help construct an animal home or dig for clues in this fun area. There's the chance for visitors to stroke a stingray and see a host of snakes, insects and lizards.

Add-on adventures at the zoo which attract a small additional fee include a train ride, kayaking, paddle boats and feeding various animals (the giraffes are particularly fun!).

There are a variety of combo tickets available offering some of these add-ons at reduced rates. Rhino Encounters, Wildlife Encounters and Behind the Scenes with a zookeeper experiences can also be arranged.

Additional Information

The latest addition to Brevard Zoo's recreational area is a 10-foot wide boardwalk that runs from the car park for just over a mile through nearby wetlands and oak hammocks.

Known as the Brevard Zoo Linear Park, this elevated recreational boardwalk is free.

Treetop Trek

Admission to the Treetop Trek is entirely separate from zoo admission. This aerial obstacle course is a self-guided adventure through the treetops using zip lines, rope bridges, crab walks, nets, tightropes and other challenges. There are five different options, depending on your height and the number of challenges you want to experience at heights ranging from 20-50 feet above the ground.

Admission and Tour

Zoo only - Adults $16.95 with concessions for seniors and children.

Treetop Trek courses from $14.95 to $64.95.

Opening Times

Open daily 9.30 a.m. to 5 p.m.

Where to Eat at Brevard Zoo

No outside food or drink is permitted in the zoo, but there are picnic tables outside the animal park.

Inside the zoo there are several places to buy reasonably priced refreshments and snacks at the Flamingo Café and Paws On Pizzeria.

Nearby Attractions

- Rossetter House Museum
- Sebastian Inlet State Park
- Island Boat Lines Tours

Daytona Beach and International Speedway

Daytona Beach is a 23-mile stretch of gorgeous golden sand running down the Atlantic coast of Florida, south of St Augustine, and just north of New Smyrna Beach.

It's a must for motorheads and those interested in touring behind the scenes at the Daytona International Speedway. It provides a great day out for those wanting to spend the day on the beach as, unlike Cocoa Beach, you can drive right onto the sand in the vehicle-accessible areas.

Daytona Beach & Pier

The city of Daytona Beach is a sizeable community with a marina, the Volusia Mall and Daytona International Speedway.

There is a good range of waterfront dining and all the usual small businesses you will find in any Florida community, from tire shops to real estate agencies, banks, liquor stores, fast food restaurants, Starbucks, Wal-Mart, Sam's Club and Walgreens. If you need anything, you will find it in Daytona Beach!

Location
Located 79 miles north of Cocoa Beach via I-95 or the coastal US-1.

Daytona International Speedway
1801 W. International Speedway Blvd
Daytona Beach
FL 32114
Tel: 1-800-748-7467 or 1-877-306-7223

www.daytonainternationalspeedway.com

What to Expect on a Visit to Daytona Beach
Daytona Beach has firmly packed sand and rolling Atlantic waves, making it ideal for surfing, sunbathing, kite-surfing or long walks in the constant breeze. There are trained lifeguards in the most popular areas of the beach with warning flags indicating beach conditions and information on the tide and temperatures. Even on the hottest day the beach is bearable if you have some shade from an umbrella and an onshore wind.

A great place for youngsters to cool off is in the Sunsplash Park, which has jet fountains and a shady undercover playground to give children a place to play in the shade.

The beach is overlooked by hotels and high-rise apartment buildings, many of which are shuttered against hurricanes as their owners visit for just a few weeks each year. The more popular buildings tend to be timeshare-owned with beautiful swimming pools and tiki bars overlooking the beach. There are some amusement parks and fun fair rides along Daytona Beach, but as you travel further south, the beach becomes quieter and is overlooked by private homes of all sizes and ages. The best thing about Daytona Beach is that for around $10 you can drive your car right onto the beach and park for the day. Vans cruise up and down selling drinks and snacks and there are regular beach patrols.

There are plenty of things to do around Daytona Beach apart from the beach and shops. Take a relaxing trip on the Halifax River to see the dolphins, birds, and wildlife. In the winter, the St John's River is where many manatees gather to feed. Alternatively, take the Daytona Trolley Bus Tour around the sights or enjoy a tour in one of the amphibious vehicles that start on the highway and then plunge into the river. The Museum of Photography and the Ormond Memorial Art Museum are also worth paying a visit.

One of the most modern entertainment areas is Ocean Walk Village at the end of Main Street. The complex has several upmarket hotels and a theater, shops, amusements, oceanfront dining, bars, and restaurants. Right across the street from Ocean Walk Village is the Convention Center,

Daytona Lagoon Waterpark and Arcade. Nearby is a children's playground, fun center, boardwalk and the pier.

The miles of firm sand on Daytona Beach gave birth to the city becoming the home of supercharged speed. The first Daytona Speedway races ran for almost 50 years on an unofficial racing circuit that included the beach and part of the A1A Highway, which runs parallel. Finally, the racing was placed on a more permanent footing when the Daytona International Speedway was built in 1959 on what became known as International Speedway Drive. The stadium has since become a landmark of the area. The track is 2½ miles long and the building of the improved circuit coincided with faster and more reliable racing cars, so the main race was increased from 200 to 500 miles in length.

When races are not in progress, visitors can take a guided tour of the huge stadium on the 480-acre site. Guides take you behind the scenes to see what is involved in making NASCAR events run smoothly.

Visitors get to see the Drivers' Meeting Room, tour the NASCAR Spring Cup Series garages, view the Victory Lane, and take a peek inside the press box, seven floors above the track itself.

Additional Information

Driving is generally allowed in the vehicle-accessible areas on Daytona Beach from one hour after sunrise to one hour before sunset. However, in the turtle nesting seasons (May 1 to Oct 31), driving hours are strictly between 8 a.m. and 7 p.m.

Drivers must stick to the driving lanes, park in the designated areas, and maintain the 10mph speed limit.

Dogs are not permitted on Daytona Beach.

Cost

The beach is free for pedestrians and cyclists, but a $10 charge is made per vehicle for parking on the sand.

Daytona International Speedway Tours Cost

Adults from $16; Children 6-12 $10 for a 30-minute Speedway Tour.

Longer VIP tours and All Access Tours are also available. Advanced reservations are recommended as places are limited.

Opening Times

Daytona International Speedway is open daily from 9 a.m. to 5 p.m.

Speedway Tours run daily at 11.30 a.m., 1.30 p.m., 3.30 p.m. and 4 p.m. Other tours are on specific days and times.

Where to Eat at Daytona Beach

A particular favorite restaurant of mine is the Hyde Park Steakhouse Restaurant in the Hilton Hotel, where you can get great deals on cocktails from 5 p.m. with small plates, lite bites and superb steaks with excellent side dishes. It is an upmarket restaurant but the deals and early bird specials make it a great value place to dine with topnotch waiter service.

For somewhere relaxed and affordable, try Caribbean Jack's Restaurant and Beach Bar on Ballough Road. It has an excellent menu and plenty of tables overlooking the Intracoastal Waterway. Live music ensures it stays busy and lively at night, but lunchtimes are quieter and very pleasant.

Nearby Attractions
- Ponce Inlet Lighthouse
- DeBary Hall
- New Smyrna Marine Discovery Center
- Blue Springs State Park
- Historic St. Augustine

Marine Discovery Center in New Smyrna Beach

Combine a day at the beach with a visit to the Marine Discovery Center. It's a real hidden gem, particularly for those wanting to amuse children with supervised and educational activities. The Science Center has daily activities such as oyster recycling, crafts and fishing, so it's well worth joining in the fun.

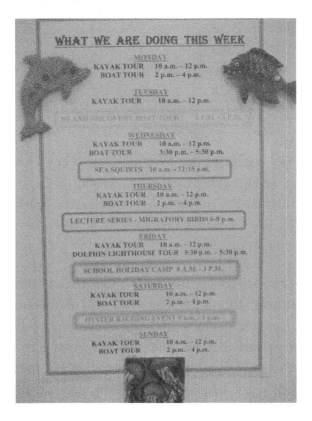

Hop aboard one of the daily boat trips, dolphin tours, guided kayak tours and hands-on adventure tours all led by certified naturalists.

Book ahead or just drop into the Marine Discovery Center any time and have fun exploring the free exhibits and touch tanks. You'll certainly want to come back for more!

Location

Located 65 miles north of Cocoa Beach on the Indian River Lagoon just north of Hwy 44.

Marine Discovery Center (MDC)
520 Barracuda Blvd
New Smyrna Beach
FL32169
Tel: (386) 428-4828

www.marinediscoverycenter.org

What to Expect at the Marine Discovery Center

The Marine Discovery Center is a wonderful reason to visit New Smyrna Beach, in conjunction with a trip to the beautiful sandy beach which you can actually drive on and park for a nominal fee.

The Marine Discovery Center is a fun place to drop in and look around for free with various observation tanks containing hermit crabs in large conch shells, horseshoe crabs semi buried in the sand, and crown conch. Children are encouraged to pull out the drawer displays and discover sea shells, sea beans, sharks' skin and other curious exhibits.

The display of sharks' teeth is certainly fascinating, along with the huge teeth of the extinct megalodon and other sea creatures.

Even more fun are the many tanks of sea creatures at the center. There are aquariums of pretty starfish, anemones, fish, crabs and other unusual sea creatures. When we visited, my children loved the sea horses that were nosing around in seaweed. The docent told us they were due to give birth. Apparently the tiny sea horses are born fully formed and well able to fend for themselves.

The rear classroom has much more to see, from colorful posters on the wall to skulls, a corn snake, an interesting shark tank and more fish. This room is used for many activities which are suitable for all ages.

The Marine Discovery Center offers 2-hour Dolphin Discovery Tours daily on a pontoon boat to see dolphins, manatees and birds in their natural habitat. There are also daily guided kayak tours with a marine specialist guide who will take you through the mangroves and backwaters for close encounters with local wildlife.

If you want to get more hands-on, the excellent Island Adventure Tours take place on the first and third Tuesday of the month. These 3-hour interactive eco tours are led by certified naturalists. With the help of sieves, dip and seine nets (and wet feet!) guests find and identify fish, conchs, sea stars, horseshoe crabs and other wildlife around the islands and sandbars of the Indian River.

Additional Info

The Marine Discovery Center is within easy reach of the charming shops, cafés, art galleries and businesses in Flagler Ave's historic homes and the Old Seaside Station.

Admission
Admission to the center and its touch tank exhibits is free.

Dolphin Discovery Tours (2 hours)
Adults $28, Seniors and Students $25, Children under 12 $12. Family ticket for 2 adults and 2 children $70.

Guided Kayak Tours (2 hours)
Adults $35, Children 6-12 $20

Island Adventure Tours (3 hours hands-on)
Adults $35; Seniors $30; Children under 12 $20

Opening Times
The Marine Discovery Center and Gift Shop is open daily 9 a.m. to 5 p.m.

Where to Eat At New Smyrna Beach
Browse the cafés and restaurants on nearby Flagler Ave or head out to the beach on Atlantic Ave. One of my favorite places to dine is Breakers, which is right on the beach on S. Atlantic Ave. There are plenty of outdoor tables so you can watch youngsters running off their energy on the firm sands or playing in the tidal pools. The restaurant is very casual and family friendly with generous portions of tasty food.

Nearby Attractions
- New Smyrna Beach
- Blue Spring State Park
- Sun Splash Park, Daytona
- Daytona International Speedway Museum

Blue Spring State Park

If you fancy seeing the amazing spectacle of more than 200 manatees in crystal clear water just yards from your feet, then head to Blue Spring State Park near DeLand. This gold award-winning state park is the winter home to more than 200 manatees that seek out the warm spring waters when the cold nights descend.

An excellent boardwalk runs beside the lagoon with frequent lookout points over the exceptional blue-green waters.

The Blue Spring Run is teeming with fish, and in the summer is ideal for swimming, snorkeling, tubing, canoeing or taking a two-hour narrated boat trip along the St Johns River.

Location

Located 88 miles northwest of Cocoa Beach near Orange City

Blue Spring State Park
2100 West French Avenue
Orange City
FL 32763
Tel: (386) 775-3663

www.floridastateparks.org/park/Blue-Spring

What to Expect on a Visit to Blue Spring State Park

Blue Spring State Park caters admirably for those who want to amble around and enjoy the natural sights. This National Gold Medal Winning State Park has superb facilities as well as being Florida's premiere manatee refuge.

The 1/3 mile-long boardwalk runs beside the Blue Spring Run through a shady hardwood hammock. The natural beauty has everyone reaching for their cameras. Listen to the gasps of surprise as eyes focus on shoals of fish and the manatees, the stars of the show, in the clear waters below.

The manatees swim into the lagoon in cold weather as the prolific Blue Spring disgorges 104 million gallons of water per day at a balmy 72°F. In contrast, the St Johns River where the manatees feed ranges from 50°F in winter to 80°F in summer.

Gazing into the spring waters from the viewing platforms is like peering into nature's aquarium. Sunfish, longnose gar, tarpon, turtles and other water-loving creatures can clearly be seen against the white sandy bottom of the shallow lagoon. The blue waters are so clear that visitors can even see the scars from boat propellers on the manatees' soft grey hide. These gentle giants can reach 9-10 feet in length and weigh up to 3000lbs, which is amazing on a strictly vegetarian diet of sea grass!

Visitors can snorkel and dive from the swimming dock to see the source of the blue spring and the cave which goes down about 120 feet.

For an even better view of the pristine springs and the wildlife, hire canoes and kayaks from the kiosk or book a three-hour guided kayaking adventure with a naturalist/guide. If tour boats are more your idea of a day out, join the twice-daily trip up the St Johns River on quiet pontoon boats for an excellent two-hour narrated tour.

Every trip is different, with alligators, fish, manatees, red-bellied turtles, wading birds, cooters and even the possibility of a black bear sighting.

Take a self-guided tour of the original 1872 Thursby House, the enviably located home of Louis Thursby and his family who settled here. A campsite, overnight cabins, children's play area and a 4-mile backwoods trail (each way) complete the excellent amenities. All you need to bring is a picnic and a bathing suit!

Additional Information
The best time to see the manatees is in winter, from November to April, and here's a tip from a volunteer warden. Visit in the morning, after a cold night, and you will see as many as 200 of these endangered creatures that have moved into the warmer spring waters from the chilly St Johns River during the night. This is a sight few people in the world are privileged enough to see, and future generations may never get the chance.

Admission
$6.00 per vehicle. Limit 2-8 people per vehicle.
$4.00 Single Occupant Vehicle.
$2.00 Pedestrians, bicyclists, extra passengers, passengers in vehicle with holder of Annual Individual Entrance Pass.

Opening Times
Open daily 8:00 a.m. until sundown.

Where to Eat near Blue Spring State Park

There are plenty of picnic tables and grassy areas for enjoying a picnic without having to leave the state park. There are also some concessions selling snacks onsite.

The best place for a restaurant meal is in DeLand, the classy county seat of Volusia. Main Street Grill is a local favorite for a meal and the Secret Garden, also on E. New York Ave, offers a delectable menu of French and international inspired cuisine.

The Boston Coffee House on New York Avenue is a good choice for coffee or lunch and the Coffee Bistro 101 does excellent iced Frappuccino just around the corner on N. Woodland Ave.

Nearby Attractions
- DeBary Hall
- Marine Discovery Center at New Smyrna Beach
- Airboat Rides at Midway

DeBary Hall

Those who enjoy seeing how the other half live will enjoy a trip to DeBary Hall, a lovely Victorian mansion listed on the National Register of Historic Places. Guided tours of this elegant home are provided by local guides. Visitors can then explore the estate on the banks of the St Johns River.

Location
Located 82 miles northwest of Cocoa Beach in the small town of DeBary, north of Sanford.

DeBary Hall
210 Sunrise Blvd
DeBary
FL32713
Tel: (386) 668-3840

www.debaryhall.com/

What to Expect on a Visit to DeBary Hall

Like many wealthy families seeking a warm respite from the New York winters, Frederick DeBary visited the east coast of Florida by steamboat in the 1870s. He had made his fortune as a wine merchant and was looking for a place to build a grand hunting estate and vacation home. He eventually acquired land on the banks of Lake Monroe and built this beautiful plantation-style home.

Guided tours of DeBary Hall offer a fascinating insight into the life of the wealthy DeBary family and give a glimpse of gracious living. The period rooms were where Mr. DeBary entertained family and friends who enjoyed riding, fishing, shooting quail and "varmint" hunting. He also tried his hand at orange growing on the 6000 acre estate and ran commercial steam boats for a time, fuelled by the 19th century tourist boom.

Once your tour of this splendid Victorian Hunting Lodge is over, head for the Visitor Center and learn all about the history of the St Johns River. There is an excellent film which includes a virtual steamboat ride. The film explains the role the St Johns River played in making Florida accessible to wealthy northern families who built winter homes and estates in Florida in the 19th century. It also gives an informative look at the life of Frederick DeBary with photographs of DeBary Hall in its heyday with its fountain and exotic gardens.

Explore the various outbuildings which are put to good use around the estate. The stables are now used as function rooms but there are still restored carriages on display in part of the building. Peek inside the worker's cottage on the estate and see the latest must-have for Victorian homes – the ice house!

If you have any energy left, trek the 2.2 mile Spring-to-Spring Trail which starts at the DeBary trailhead pavilion. The estate also has a shady picnic area and a well-stocked gift shop.

Additional Information
Special interest tours at DeBary Hall can be booked with 2 weeks' notice and are ideal for Red Hats groups and special interest clubs. Topics include an Architecture Tour, an Ecological Tour and a Tea Time Tour, which includes an elegant tea-tasting experience.

Admission and Tour
Adults $5 with special rates for seniors and children under 12.

Opening Times
Open Tuesday to Saturday 10 a.m. to 4 p.m. Sunday noon to 4p.m.

Where to Eat near DeBary Hall
DeBary Hall is sadly lacking an on-site tearoom but staff will direct visitors into the small town of DeBary, which has several restaurants and cafés.

My personal preference is to head out to New Smyrna Beach (East on DeBary Ave and Doyle Road to Hwy 415 then north to pick up Hwy 44 East until you reach the beach, about 30 miles from DeBary). You can then drive south on the A1A and pick one of the waterfront bars overlooking the ocean or the intracoastal waterway for a pleasant drink and a reasonably priced meal with great waterfront views.

Nearby Attractions

- Mount Dora
- New Smyrna Beach
- Blue Heron River Tours at DeLand

Veteran's Park in nearby Sanford

Winter Park Scenic Boat Tour

Many locals have never heard of this memorable boat trip at Winter Park, which is a hidden gem. The narrated cruises cross Lake Osceola and enter Lake Virginia via an inter-connecting canal. It's a great trip for birdwatching and the commentary includes light-hearted information about the area, local history and wildlife. As well as seeing some beautiful waterfront homes, the cruise includes sights of Rollins College Campus, Kraft Azalea Park and Lake Maitland.

Winter Park Scenic Boat Tour

There is plenty of free parking near the boat dock. Buy your ticket early and then go for a stroll around nearby Winter Park. When the boat is loaded, parties are called by name in the order they bought the tickets, so early ticket-buyers get to pick the best seats.

Location

Located 63 miles west of Cocoa Beach in northeast Orlando.

Scenic Boat Tour
312 East Morse Blvd
Winter Park
FL32789
Tel: (407) 644-4056

http://www.scenicboattours.com/

What to Expect on a Scenic Boat Tour in Winter Park

This one-hour cruise explores the natural beauty of the lakes and canals around historic Winter Park. The pontoon boats are very stable and suitable for the shallower waters in the canals which connect the lakes, but they have no awning to protect from the sun (or the showers!) due to the low bridges. Bench seats are provided for around 18 passengers.

The ticket office stands on the edge of the lake and opens just before the first trip of the day at 10 a.m. It is advisable to buy your ticket as early as possible to get a good seat. Benches under a canopy are provided whilst you wait for the boat to arrive. The boat skippers are excellent narrators and give a good spiel about the sights and wildlife, tell a few corny jokes and will happily answer any questions.

The boat trip begins on Lake Osceola where there are many multi-million dollar homes along the shores. After navigating through the interconnecting canal, the trip continues around Lake Virginia. The lake is shared with other boats, fishermen, jet skis and even a water-skier or two. Expect to see plenty of birds such as blue herons, which were nesting in the trees during my early-April trip. There are egrets, ducks and ducklings, anhingas, little blue herons and even osprey living in the live oaks which hang over the lake. Bougainvillea, sleeping hibiscus and plenty of bamboo add to the natural interest.

The exclusive Rollins College campus is spread along the edge of Lake Virginia with some fine buildings. The history of this famous college is the source of some interesting facts and anecdotes.

The return boat ride includes traversing Lake Osceola along the eastern shore and navigating through the winding Venetian Canal before Lake Maitland opens out before you. The Kraft Azalea Park is a picture of colorful blooms in early spring. Enjoy viewing the beautiful gardens and multi-million dollar mansions which are the winter homes of wealthy American families.

Additional Information

The boats are open to the elements so it's a good idea to bring a sunhat and/or a light raincoat depending on the season.

After a most enjoyable hour the trip ends back at the dock and you probably feel in need of refreshment. Park Avenue in Winter Park is a short walk from the lake and offers a delightful choice of upmarket shops and cafés in which to browse and dine. Across the road are the Amtrak station and a beautiful park with fountains, a scented rose garden and a pergola. This is where you will find the delightful Farmers' Market on Saturday mornings.

Admission and Tour
Adults $12 and Children (2-11) $6.00

Tours Times
Boat Tours run Monday to Sunday 10 a.m. to 4 p.m.

The scenic boat tour leaves the dock hourly and at peak times two or three boats run, so you should easily be able to turn up and secure a seat.

Where to Eat near Winter Park Boat Tour
Plan to take an 11 a.m. boat tour and enjoy lunch afterwards in nearby Winter Park. Stroll along Morse Boulevard a couple of hundred yards from the boat dock towards Winter Park's charming center and you will pass Croissant Gourmet. Coffee and cold drinks, hot stuffed croissants and a delicious array of French pastries tempt you to sit at one of their indoor or curbside tables. A decadent treat, but worth it.

Just around the corner in Park Avenue there are a number of restaurants which spill onto the sidewalk, including the Bistro on Park Avenue and 310 Park South. They are all well-priced for lunch and are obviously very popular.

Nearby Attractions
- Charles Hosmer Morse Museum of American Art with its fine collection of Tiffany Glass
- Kraft Azalea Gardens on Lake Maitland
- Harry P. Leu Gardens

Gatorland

If you want to do something completely different and authentically Floridian, spend the day at Gatorland on S. Orange Blossom Trail (US 17/441). I was so impressed on my afternoon visit that I would have gone there sooner had I known just how much it had to offer!

As well as the expected pools of alligators, there is a veritable zoo of animals, from emus and giant tortoises to flamingoes, owls, parrots and deer. There is also a petting zoo, boardwalk, train ride, fantastic Screamin' Gator zip line adventure, splashzone and three excellent animal shows. It's the perfect day out for families of all ages.

Location

Located 61 miles east of Cocoa Beach, on Hwy 441 near Kissimmee.

Gatorland
14501 S. Orange Blossom Trail
Orlando
FL32837
Tel: (407) 855-5496 or (800) 393-5297

http://www.gatorland.com/

What to Expect on a Visit to Gatorland

Newly rebuilt in 2008, the park at Gatorland is attractively laid out and well maintained. Your first photo opportunity will be at the entrance, which is a giant walk-through alligator jaw!

The first sight, after passing through the gift shop and ticket office, is two large lakes which seem to be a mass of alligator bodies. There are different sized gators and crocodiles in various other pools nearby. Kids will enjoy buying some special food and throwing it to the alligators to see their snapping jaws. The lakes are actually big enough to have islands and one is home to a colony of pretty pink flamingos.

Along the main drag there are a series of animal exhibits in outdoor displays or aquariums. Look out for Sandhill cranes, Burmese pythons, a truly giant tortoise and a wide range of other snakes, animals and birds in cornily named areas such as the Very Merry Aviary and Allie's Barnyard. The nice surprise here is that visitors can go into the pen and touch/stroke the barnyard animals and even handle the lorikeets that fly down for food. The snakes, fortunately, were well secured behind glass.

After riding around the park on the Choo-Choo Express, head for the long raised boardwalk through the native Cypress Swamp. It's a really nice area for walking beside a naturalized lake area. This is the Breeding Marsh and Bird

Rookery where 130 adult gators live in the 10-acre wetland environment. Everywhere you look you will see alligator eyes watching unblinkingly. The accompanying fact boards do a good job of informing you of the breeding habits of alligators, and actual identify some of the reptiles by their territory, size or individual characteristics.

Daring visitors can climb the Observation Tower and strap their harness to the Screamin' Gator Zipline, under careful instruction from the trainer. Then you're off, flying high above the greenery and water as you go from platform to platform.

The Splash Zone is a great place for youngsters to cool off with many jets, flumes and water features.

It's worth hanging around for the last show of the day, the Gator Jumparoo Show. The entertainment includes a routine between a trainer and two sidekicks who were allegedly auditioning as would-be trainers. The alligators circle in the water, clearly knowing food is due and eventually they jump high into the area to snap at a whole chicken. They make quite a splash!

The other excellent shows which take place throughout the day include Gator Wrestling, where wranglers do a series of stunts, and there's an Upclose Encounters Show where some of Florida's more unusual wildlife is displayed and talked about by trained staff.

All-in-all Gatorland is a really enjoyable Florida-themed attraction that I can highly recommend to families of all ages.

Additional Information
Parking at the attraction is free.

Additional events at Gatorland include the Gator Night Shine after dark, or the chance to be a Trainer for a Day.

Admission
Adults $26.99 Children (3-12) $18.99

Special packages and discounts are available online

Opening Times
Open daily 10 a.m. to 5 p.m.

Where to Eat at Gatorland
There is affordable hot food at Pearl's Smokehouse including burgers, pulled pork sandwiches and even fried gator nuggets! There's also a general store and a coffee shop onsite.

Alternatively, bring a picnic and make use of the attraction's picnic tables.

Nearby Attractions
- Forever Florida horseback rides
- Kissimmee Swamp Airboat Tours

Airboat Rides at Midway

Explore the Central Florida Everglades on an exciting and informative airboat ride. Glide through the marshes, see an Indian Burial Mound and explore an ancient Cypress forest. The trip includes sightings of turtles, blue herons, bald eagles, other water birds and alligators in their natural setting.

Guests are provided with two-way headsets, making it easy to communicate and ask questions above the noisy roar of the airboat engine. It's a fantastic trip combining Florida wildlife sightings with a thrilling airboat experience, and every eco tour is different.

Location
Located 40 miles from Cocoa Beach on East Highway 50.

Airboat Rides at Midway
28501 East Colonial Drive
Christmas
FL 32709
Tel: (407) 568-6790

www.airboatridesatmidway.com

What to Expect on a Visit to Airboat Rides at Midway

Launched from their own floating marina, Airboat Rides at Midway explore the flowing waters of the St Johns River as it winds its way through the Everglades of Central Florida. This family-owned and operated airboat company has been in business in Orange County since the 1930s.

The highly maneuverable airboats are noisy but they are ideal for navigating shallow water areas and floating islands of grass. Tiered bench seating ensures everyone has a great view of the wildlife you will encounter on your airboat adventure.

The airboats can zip across the still waters at speeds of up to 25mph and spin through 180 degrees to go back and check any interesting sightings. These shallow-drafted crafts can silently glide up close to watch birds, turtles or alligators lying in the sun, providing an excellent opportunity to see and photograph Florida wildlife at its best.

The customized airboats are captained by licensed US Coast Guard Master Captains who also provide endless information about the wildlife you will encounter during your tour. You will also learn about the history and ecology of this swampy wilderness, making it a truly memorable and unforgettable trip. Your experienced local guide will point out and identify wildlife and will be happy to answer any questions.

The waterways are lined with old-growth cypress trees draped in grey Spanish moss which are home to many birds of prey including bald eagles and ospreys. Blue herons, egrets, ibis, limpkins and other water birds wade through the shallows looking for food, while predatory alligators can be seen basking in the sun or swimming on the surface looking for unsuspecting prey. Other wildlife to keep an eye open for are turtles, otters, frogs and nesting birds.

Once your one-hour eco tour is over, there's the chance to hold a baby gator for photographs. You can also see exotic birds, parrots, a Burmese python and snakes at the wildlife exhibit inside the mural-covered Gift Shop. This is the place to pick up Florida souvenirs of your memorable airboat tour and buy refreshments.

Additional Information

Airboat Rides at Midway offer private airboat tours and Night Tours for up to 6 guests. They also offer seasonal Gator Hunts.

Cost

Adults $40; Children 4-12 $30

Tour Times

Open daily. First ride is at 9.30 a.m. and hourly thereafter.

Advance reservations recommended.

Where to Eat near Airboat Rides at Midway

There are no places for lunch at Christmas, but the junction with the I-95 about four miles east has a selection of chain restaurants including Taco Bell, McDonald's, Panda Express and Subway. Alternatively continue on into the Orlando suburbs.

Nearby Attractions

- Fort Christmas Historical Park
- Enchanted Forest
- Kennedy Space Center

Kennedy Space Center Visitor Complex

Kennedy Space Center is a full day out with dozens of exhibits, IMAX theaters and experiences based on the fascinating history of U.S. space travel to date. It is the perfect attraction for adults and older children with an interest in space exploration.

The Visitor Complex attracts over 1.5 million visitors annually and offers the chance to touch a moon rock, walk beneath the largest rocket ever launched, meet a NASA astronaut, experience the International Space Station and get up-close to the Space Shuttle *Atlantis,* which was retired from service in 2011.

Kennedy Space Center

Location
Located 23 miles north of Cocoa Beach on Merritt Island.

Access is from N. Courtenay Pkwy (Hwy-3) or Nasa Pkwy West.

Tel: 1-866-737-5235

www.kennedyspacecenter.com

What to Expect on a Visit to Kennedy Space Center (KSC)
General Admission tickets include an informative 1-1.5 hour Bus Tour around the extensive site complex. View the launch pad, marvel at the 363-foot long Saturn V Rocket and enjoy an informative commentary. Other bus tours, for those interested in a more in-depth tour of the KSC landmarks and space history, require an additional ticket.

Space Shuttle Atlantis
This state-of-the-art exhibit features multimedia presentation and over 60 interactive exhibits for would-be astronauts and science lovers to try out. High-tech simulators bring the complex space systems vividly to life in this 21st century exhibit.

Shuttle Launch Experience
This popular virtual launch experience takes visitors through pre-flight checks and explains the various processes taken by astronauts aboard NASA's Space Shuttle. Visitors then enter the "shuttle," are strapped in, and prepare for blast-off in this virtual space shuttle launch.

It is a fun experience and, despite the serious and frightening warnings beforehand, I found it was actually quite a tame but informative experience.

Astronaut Encounter

Twice a day, currently at 11 a.m. and 4 p.m., visitors can meet a former astronaut face-to-face. The session lasts 25 minutes and takes place within the Information Central building.

IMAX Theater 3D Films (2 locations)

Journey to Space – A 3D film showing NASA's plans for landing astronauts on Mars and capturing asteroids. Interviews with astronauts cover the past, present and future of space exploration.

Hubble 3D – A 43-minute film which will change your view of our universe as you float alongside space-walking astronauts and see the legacy of the powerful Hubble telescope. It features a compilation of Hubble images of deep space discovery.

Rocket Garden

Laid out around an outdoor garden area are various replica rockets and capsules from former space expeditions including Titan II and the 223-foot long Saturn 1B.

Climb inside the cramped quarters of capsules from the Mercury, Gemini and Apollo eras. Read the informative panels or join one of the free guided tours (currently at 9.30 a.m., 10.15 a.m., 4.45 p.m. and 5.30 p.m.)

History of Space Exploration

See the actual Mercury Mission Control consoles and other space artifacts now superseded by more modern technology.

Astronaut Memorial

A space mirror honoring the names of astronauts lost in the cause of space exploration – a sobering thought.

Children's Play Dome

A space-themed play area for young astronauts under 48 inches tall.

Journey to Mars

A live presentation every 30 minutes in NASA Central Plaza where participants can learn what it takes to be part of future space travel.

Astronaut Hall of Fame

General admission tickets include 2-day admission to the Astronaut Hall of Fame (within 7 days of visit). The Astronaut Hall of Fame is at a separate location 6 miles west of the KSC visitor complex on the approach road to the Kennedy Space Center.

This interactive experience allows visitors to try out some of the training and G-force simulators to see if you have what it takes to join the space program. It also includes the world's largest collection of astronaut memorabilia and the chance to ride a rover across rocky Mars terrain, making it a very interesting bonus to your KSC visit.

Add-On Options to Admission Tickets

KSC Up-Close Tour

This behind-the-scenes 2-hour guided tour is narrated by a space program expert who imparts little-known facts as you visit the Space Shuttle Launch Pads A and B, the Vehicle Assembly Building, the Shuttle Landing Facility, Crawlerway and Crawler Transporter that transported the space shuttle from the VAB to the launch pad.

Lunch with an Astronaut

This is one of the most popular programs, giving visitors of all ages the chance to meet over lunch with a member of NASA's Astronaut team, ask questions and get their autograph. This personalized presentation by a featured astronaut describes what it is like to live and work in space.

Special Viewing for Rocket Launches

Rockets continue to be launched from the Kennedy Space Center. Dates are published in advance on the KSC website so you can plan your visit to include viewing one of these launches from the Apollo/Saturn V Center.

For an additional fee, you can view rocket launches live from bleacher seating near the Space Shuttle Atlantis, the LC-39 Observation Gantry or the NASA Causeway. You will certainly feel the rocket's rumble and hear the engines roar from these privileged viewing locations.

Admission

Adult Admission $50; Children $40

Lunch with an Astronaut add-on

Adults	$29.99
Children 3-11	$15.99

Prices for other tours and activities can be found on the KSC website.

Opening Times

Open daily 9 a.m. to 6 p.m. (later closing during the summer). Closed Christmas Day.

Where to Eat at the Kennedy Space Center

There are numerous refreshments areas for purchasing everything from an ice cream to a full lunch.

Orbit Café has something for all tastes while the Moon Rock Café at the Apollo/Saturn V Center offers a choice of dining accompanied by the recreated sights and sounds of an Apollo lunar landing as part of your visit.

Light refreshments are also available at the LC-39 Observation Gantry, the Milky Way and the G-Force Grill.

The ultimate dining opportunity is the chance to have lunch with veteran NASA astronaut and hear exciting personal accounts of space exploration. There is also time for questions and photos.

Nearby Attractions

- Island Boat Lines Eco Tours
- Air Force Space and Missile Museum Tour
- Airboat Rides at Midway

Tour of Cape Canaveral Air Force Station and Lighthouse

Most people interested in space travel will want to spend a day at the Kennedy Space Center during their stay on Florida's Space Coast. However, there is another way to take a tour and learn more about American space history.

The 45th Space Wing of the Patrick Air Force Base (AFB) conducts free public tours by bus around the Cape Canaveral Air Force Station, Air Force Space and Missile Museum, several launch pads and the historic Cape Canaveral Lighthouse. The only catch is that these 3-hour guided tours are very popular, so you need to book at least 60 days ahead of your planned visit.

Location
The Air Force Space and Missile Museum is located 7 miles north of Cocoa Beach at Cape Canaveral Air Force Station

Air Force Space and Missile Museum
100 Spaceport Way
Cape Canaveral
FL 32920
Tel: (321) 853-1919 or (321) 494-5945 for tour information

www.patrick.af.mil/tourprogram.asp

http://afspacemuseum.org/

What to Expect on the Tour

Tours start at the History Center on Complex 26, Cape Canaveral Air Force Station. Guests are asked to be present at 8.30 a.m. to check in and run through a final security check. Your tour guides will be two civilian employees from the 45th Space Wing, which is responsible for delivered assured space launch, range and combat capabilities for the nation.

It's an amazing chance to be able to see "behind the scenes" of these operations with these dedicated professionals, who provide an informative commentary and are always happy to answer your questions. At each stop on the tour there are opportunities to explore and take photographs, so definitely bring a camera to record your historic visit

Rocket Garden

The History Center is part of the Air Force Space and Missile Museum and has exhibits about the different launch pads and complexes onsite. After a short talk, the tour progresses to the main part of the Air Force Space and Missile Museum. Here you will see many fascinating displays of different missiles, rockets and other space equipment. The museum continually collects, restores and displays items of historical interest, building up a fascinating collection of items that accurately depict the history and development of the US space launch activities.

The Space and Missile Museum is near Launch Complexes 5 and 6. Older visitors may remember the first manned sub-orbital Mercury capsule, *Freedom 7,* which was launched with Alan Shepard onboard in 1961. He became the first American in space and holds an important place in space history. After flying for 15 minutes 28 seconds at an altitude of 116.5 miles, the spacecraft landed in the Atlantic Ocean to complete a successful first mission.

The bus then transports visitors to see the retired and active launch pads used for Delta 4 launches, such as the Launch Complex 37B. More history unfolds at the Launch Complex 26 blockhouse which housed two firing rooms for dual pads. Built in 1956, the walls are two feet thick and the domed roof is almost eight feet thick to withstand the firing and launch of the first American satellite, *Explorer 1.* It is now a National Historic Landmark and has several displays and a small satellite.

You can still see much of the original equipment, computers and clocks which look extremely clunky and outdated compared to modern communications.

Other significant locations on the tour include Launch Complex 14, from where astronaut John Glenn was launched and became the first American to orbit the earth. This was also where President John F. Kennedy announced plans that America would land men on the moon. Launch Complex 34 was the launch site of Apollo 7, the last human space flight to take place from the Air Force Station. Launch Complex 37 was the launch site for the Delta IV Expendable Launch Vehicle program.

A moving part of the tour is at Launch Complex 34, where Gus Grissom, Ed White and Roger B. Chafee lost their lives in 1967 in a fire during a pre-launch test. The launch platform remains as a tribute to the astronauts of Apollo 1 and a plaque is attached to the structure.

Next stop is the Rocket Garden inside the Kennedy Space Center grounds. These massive exhibits record past missile programs in a tangible way. They bring home just how perilous, cramped and basic the early manned spaceships were.

During the final part of the tour, the bus heads north of the base to the historic Cape Canaveral Lighthouse. This lighthouse was the second to be built on the cape, replacing the original 1848 structure with a new steel tower in 1868. The lighthouse is unusual as the lighthouse keeper and his family actually lived in the lower three levels of the lighthouse. It had an exterior staircase for climbing up the 151-foot structure to maintain the Fresnel lens.

The distinctive black and white bands were created in 1873 to identify the lighthouse. Visitors will hear how the lighthouse was moved in the 1890s as erosion threatened it. It only became automated in 1967 and was incorporated into the Space and Missile Museum in 1995. It is the only operational lighthouse to be owned by the U.S. Air Force.

Additional Information

Security is high at this operational Air Force Station and some visitors must submit personal information for security clearance before the tour can be taken. This applies to adults who are not Florida residents, guests under the age of 17 and non-US citizens. Approved guests must produce two forms of official ID when arriving for their tour.

Wear comfortable walking shoes and bring a camera and bottled water.

Tour Cost

Free.

You should submit the online tour application form on the official website of Patrick Air Force Base at least 60 days prior to your planned visit. Alternatively, send an email request to: ccafstours@us.af.mil

Tour Times

Tours are offered on Wednesdays and Thursdays at 9 a.m., excluding dates when there are launch missions, military exercises or federal holidays.

The Air Force Space and Missile History Center is also open to the public free at the following times:

Tuesday to Friday from 9 a.m. to 2 p.m., Saturday 9 a.m. to 5 p.m. and Sunday from noon to 4 p.m.

Where to Eat near Cape Canaveral Air Force Station

There are several places to eat on the aptly named Satellite Beach, just south of the Patrick AFB. For breakfast before your tour, try Beachside Bagel World or the Banana River Café, both on S. Patrick Drive.

Neighboring Surfs Up Café at the Lori Laine Shopping Center serves outstanding home cooked food, salads, soup and sandwiches all day.

Nearby Attractions
- Kennedy Space Center
- Astronaut Hall of Fame
- Sebastian Inlet State Park

Island Boat Lines Eco Tour

The excellent two-hour Island Boat Lines Eco Tour sets off in search of Florida wildlife on a stable pontoon boat which cruises around the barrier islands of the Banana River in the Indian River Lagoon.

Tours are led by a USCG certified Captain and a professional naturalist, who both do a terrific job spotting and identifying wildlife, providing a host of information and a few smiles along the way. It is a most pleasant way to spend a couple of hours relaxing and is a great opportunity to photograph Florida birds, alligators and marine life in its natural habitat.

Location

Located on the E. Merritt Island Causeway/West Cocoa Beach Causeway (Hwy 520). The jetty is outside the Sunset Waterfront Grill and Bar.

Island Boat Lines Eco Tour
500 West Cocoa Beach Causeway
Cocoa Beach
FL32931
Tel: (800) 979-3370 or (321) 454-7414

www.islandboatlines.com

What to Expect on an Island Boat Lines Eco Tour

After checking in at the Sunset Waterfront Grill, take your seat aboard the colorful pontoon boat with its shady awning. The boats sail smoothly and quietly through the clear waters of the Thousand Islands area of the Indian River Lagoon. This peaceful area is part of the Inter Coastal Waterway which runs up Florida's East Coast.

The clear waters in the lagoon are on average 3½ feet deep, making it very easy to spot dolphins, manatees and alligators in the brackish waters.

Barely had the boat left the dock than we saw manatees feeding close by. The captain switched off the engines and we drifted silently to get a closer look. There are about 5000 endangered manatees that live in the bay and sadly many are killed or carry the scars of encounters with boat propellers, hence the speed restrictions.

Left unharmed, manatees live for up to 60 years and exist on a vegetation diet. It's fascinating to sail close to these enormous creatures, known as sea cows. Although capable of moving at up to 15 mph, they generally swim very slowly as they graze on sea grass. The naturalist will give you plenty of facts about manatees such as that they need water temperatures of at least 68°F to survive. They carry their unborn baby for 13 months and when born it weighs around 40 pounds.

After watching manatees and other wildlife sightings, the tour moves on in the delightful calm lagoon waters which are lined with houses and low-rise apartment blocks on one side and islands on the other. The trees and bushes on the islets are home to all types of waterbirds including cormorants with their hooked beaks, herons, egrets, osprey and even kingfishers. In the breeding season the trees bear huge pelicans' nests and the heads of baby birds can be seen high in the trees.

Other wildlife you are likely to spot as part of your thrilling wildlife tour include frogs, turtles and alligators of all sizes. In spring theses toothy predators hang around beneath the nests hoping to catch a misplaced egg or baby fledgling.

The two-hour trip passes very quickly with informative dialogues from the naturalist guide. At times the captain plays cheery background music as everyone relaxes and enjoys the sights of this beautiful lagoon area.

Additional Information
Advance reservations are required.

Tour Prices
Adults $28 with concessions for seniors and children.

Tours Times
Tours operate Monday to Saturday at 10 a.m. and 2 p.m. Sunday 2 p.m. tours only.

Where to Eat near DeBary Hall
The boat drops guests right on the steps of the Sunset Waterfront Grill and Bar which serves everything from cold drinks to a competitively priced menu of salads, sandwiches, burgers and seafood.

Start or finish your trip with lunch here and note they offer all eco tour customers a discount on food and drinks. Sit on the outdoor deck overlooking the lagoon or cool off in the air-conditioned dining room.

For more upmarket food and service, try the Florida Seafood Bar and Grill on the Cocoa Beach Causeway (520) a little further east.

Nearby Attractions
- Ron Jon's Surf Shop
- Kennedy Space Center
- Brevard Zoo

Forever Florida Horseback Safari

Just 40 minutes south of the villa subdivisions of Kissimmee there is another Florida where huge lakes, scrub and sand pine forests are home to black bears, pumas, alligators, bobcats, bald-headed eagles and amazing birdlife. One of the best ways to see Florida-in-the-raw is on horseback, exploring the wildlife conservation area at Crescent J Ranch.

Location
Located 54 miles east of Cocoa Beach in St Cloud.

Forever Florida/Crescent J Ranch
4755 N Kenansville Road
St Cloud
FL 34773
Tel: 1-866-85-4EVER (1-866-854-3837)

http://foreverflorida.com

What to Expect on a Visit to Forever Florida

Forever Florida offers a variety of fully guided adventures through this managed conservation area which covers 4,700 acres of untamed wilderness. As well as horseback safaris, there is a zipline safari course or the chance to ride five feet above the swamp on an open-sided coach safari with great views of the Florida ecosystems and wildlife. Forever Florida is dedicated to reinvesting a percentage of its profits back into sustaining the wildlife and untamed environment.

Arriving at the Crescent J Ranch there is ample car parking near the Visitor Center. Check in at the shop/restaurant building where waivers must be signed and restrooms are available. You can relax in rocking chairs on the shady porch to await the arrival of your experienced guide who will take you across a meadow to the stables where a variety of well-fed horses will be pulling at their hay nets in the breezy loose boxes.

Once everyone is matched up with suitable mounts, the horseback ride sets off along dusty trails first ridden 500 years ago by Native American Indians. No doubt the landscape was much the same then – saw palmettos and sabal palms rising above the flat scrub with low shrubs and the odd flowering weed.

Riding past the small lakes the watchful eyes of an alligators can be seen silently staring back. Other wildlife includes squirrels, white-tail deer, raccoons, wild turkeys and plenty of other birds. Along the way, your guide will point out some of the highlights – huge deer feeders to sustain the wildlife through the drought, the tracks of black bears or the occasional bird of prey soaring high above.

The comfortable western saddle and relaxed pace make this a most enjoyable and pleasant ride through Florida's outback. You will ride through a sand pine forest and in the shallow headwaters of Bull Creek, which is no doubt cooling for the horses' hot and dusty hooves. During the ride there's a break and your guide will hand out chilled bottles of water and answer questions.

A horseback safari at Forever Florida is a wonderfully relaxed way to experience the natural flora and fauna of Florida, riding at one with nature.

Additional Information

You can combine your horseback ride with one of the other activities offered by Forever Florida, such as the Zipline Safaris. Allow four hours to navigate the seven ziplines and two skybridges with an experienced guide at heights of 55 feet through three separate ecosystems.

Alternatively, take a Wild Coach Safari through the area, spotting wildlife from the open-sided vehicle which carries passengers high above the swampland and bush.

Reservations are required for all activities. Call 1-866-854-3837.

Cost

90-minute Horseback Safari	$69.99
4-hour Zipline Safari	$79.99
2-hour Coach Safari Adults	$24.99
2-hour Coach Safari Children 6-12	$14.99

Opening Times

Open daily from 9 a.m. to 5 p.m.

Top Tips for Horseback Riding at Forever Florida

- Wear a shady hat or a riding helmet to keep the sun off your face
- Loose long-sleeved shirts are a good idea, or wear sunscreen on your arms
- Wear jeans or trousers to avoid legs being chafed
- Trainers or shoes with covered toes are advisable

Where to Eat at Forever Florida

The onsite Cypress Restaurant serves family favorites from 11 a.m. daily. After you've worked up a hunger on the ranch, try the BBQ pulled pork sandwich, tasty custom burgers or a freshly prepared grilled chicken salad.

Nearby Attractions

- Kissimmee Swamp Tours
- Gatorland
- Island Boat Tours

Gillian Birch

OVER TO YOU!

If you enjoyed this book of *Days Out Around Cocoa Beach* and would like to recommend it to others, please consider **POSTING A SHORT REVIEW** on Amazon or on your favorite book review site.

Your honest opinion is truly appreciated by the author and helps other readers to judge the book fairly before buying it.

Thank you so much!

.

Gillian Birch

OTHER TITLES

Look out for more books by Gillian Birch in this popular series:

- Days Out in Central Florida from The Villages
- Favorite Days Out in Central Florida from The Villages Residents
- Days Out from The Villages with Grandkids
- Days Out Around Orlando
- Days Out Around Fort Myers
- Days Out Around Clearwater & St Pete Beach
- 20 Best Florida Beaches and Coastal Cities (Also available in color)
- 20 Best Historic Homes in Florida (Also available in color)

COMING SOON

- Days Out Around Naples
- Days Out Around Orlando with Children
- Days Out in Central Florida for Active Seniors
- Days Out Around Sarasota and Bradenton
- Days Out Around Venice
- 20 Best Gardens in Florida

These will all be available shortly in paperback and ebook format.

Keep up with future publications at: www.gillianbirch.com

Gillian Birch

ABOUT THE AUTHOR

Gillian Birch is a freelance travel writer and part-time Florida resident. As the wife of a Master Mariner, she has traveled extensively and lived in some exotic locations all over the world, including Europe, the Far East, and the Republic of Panama. Her love of writing led her to keep detailed journals which are a valuable source of eye-witness information for her many published magazine articles and destination reviews.

Describing herself as having "endless itchy feet and an insatiable wanderlust," she continues to explore Florida and further afield, writing about her experiences with wonderful clarity and attention to detail.

Gillian has a Diploma from the British College of Journalism and is proud to be a member of the International Travel Writers' Alliance and the Gulf Coast Writers' Association.

Made in the USA
Las Vegas, NV
02 March 2023

68403861R00056